D0476556

THIS PAMPHLET IS TO BE
INCLUDED IN THE EMERGENCY
PACKS OF AIRCRAFT OPERATING
OVER THE SEA

# SEA
# SURVIVAL

A.M. PAMPHLET 224

PENGUIN BOOKS

PENGUIN BOOKS

UK | USA | Canada | Ireland | Australia
India | New Zealand | South Africa

Penguin Books is part of the Penguin Random House group of companies
whose addresses can be found at global.penguinrandomhouse.com.

First published by the Air Ministry 1953
First published in Penguin Books 2017
001

The moral right of the author has been asserted
Photo of RAF Gibraltar on p.40 © RAF Museum
Photo of RAF Changi on p.41 © Charles Biggadike
Photo of RAF Gan on p.42 © Richard Harcourt
Photo of RAF Christmas Island on p.43 © RAF Museum

Printed in Great Britain by Clays Ltd, St Ives plc

A CIP catalogue record for this book is available from the British Library

ISBN: 978–1–405–93165–6

www.greenpenguin.co.uk

# SEA SURVIVAL

# SEA SURVIVAL

## INTRODUCTION

1. Survival at sea for days, perhaps weeks, in difficult conditions, is a possibility facing all aircrew who fly over the sea. The fate of a crew is usually settled in the first few hours after ditching, and survival depends on two vitally important factors :—

(a) *Morale.* This is the first essential to survival in any circumstances ; without it no amount of material aid will suffice. Morale is made up of will-power and determination to live, good crew discipline, and good leadership.

(b) *Knowledge.* A thorough knowledge is required of :—

(i) Emergency drills. These should be practised for all possible contingencies until they become instinctive.

(ii) The principles of survival and the use of emergency equipment.

(iii) Emergency signals procedures.

(iv) Search and rescue organization.

If possible, the salient points of emergency drills and survival should be covered in the pre-flight briefing, especially when passengers are being carried.

## DITCHING, DINGHY, PARACHUTE, AND SWIMMING DRILLS

2. It is not within the scope of this pamphlet to discuss emergency drills in detail (A.M. Pamphlet 212, "Emergency Drills", deals fully with this subject) ; in fact, it is assumed that a safe alighting has been made in the sea by ditching or by parachute. However, knowledge of emergency drills is such a vital link in all survival, that, for the guidance of all captains of aircraft and crew members, a number of important points and often fatal mistakes are included below.

3. *Ditching and Dinghy Drills*. Ditching and dinghy drills are carefully calculated, and are not hit-or-miss affairs. Drills vary with aircraft, but the following points should always be considered :—

    (a) Number and size of exits.

    (b) Number of crew.

    (c) Type and stowage of dinghies and emergency equipment.

    (d) Previous information gained from model or actual ditchings.

Experience has shown that most multi-engined aircraft break up aft of the main spar, so crews should be placed forward if possible. Wireless operators' and navigators' ditching positions should be near their place of work, since they are working up to the last minute. Rear gunners should not be left in their turrets.

4. *Dangers Attendant upon Ditching.* Dangers can be summarized under three headings :—

    (a) Injury on impact.

    (b) Failure to escape.

    (c) Failure to survive.

5. *Injury on Impact.* Providing the pilot can execute a reasonable ditching no one need suffer any injury. Injuries are usually caused by the person failing to brace correctly, or through not knowing his drill. Injury may also result from loose or incorrect stowage, or inadequately stressed equipment within the aircraft fuselage. Therefore :—

    (a) Know how to brace. You can withstand 10g, or even more, if correctly braced.

    (b) Know your ditching stations.

    (c) Stay braced until the aircraft stops. Wait for the second impact as the nose hits the water.

6. *Failure to Escape.* Purely the fault of bad dinghy drill, such as :—

    (a) No exits open.

    (b) All trying to get out at once.

    (c) Pilot has left bomb doors open.

    (d) A lower hatch is not locked and the aircraft sinks quickly.

7. **Failure to Survive.** The initial causes are :—
   - (a) Faulty drill.
   - (b) Faulty signals procedure.
   - (c) Failure to understand the emergency.

At the first sign of trouble the captain must initiate the correct difficulty, emergency, or distress procedure ; the more information the controller receives the more efficient is his search.

8. **Personal Precautions.** If possible, do not ditch wearing a collar or tie. Make sure that your life-saving waistcoat is serviceable and inflate it with one breath only. Inflation may not be advisable, however, in aircraft with small exits.

9. **Ditching Positions.**
   - (a) Facing aft, back braced against bulkhead in a seated crouched position, knees bent and hands clasped behind the neck to prevent neck injury.
   - (b) In certain aircraft where seats are near emergency hatches it may be advisable to remain in the seat, relying on the stressing of the harness to afford protection. If facing forward, the head should be cradled for protection in the arms or in a seat cushion against a suitable support, such as a table. Rear facing seats are the best. Violent decelerations should be guarded against.
   - (c) If neither of the above positions is practicable, the deceleration may be guarded against by lying braced transversely across the fuselage floor, or flat on the floor facing forward with feet braced against a support with the knees bent.
   - (d) One man is always to be in inter-communication with the pilot.

10. **Parachute Drills.** These are laid down for each aircraft to enable crews to clear aircraft quickly and efficiently, and are based on :—
   - (a) The shortest and quickest means of getting to escape hatches.
   - (b) The even distribution in the use of escape hatches.
   - (c) The best sequence for personnel in using hatches.
   - (d) The best method of jumping to clear internal and external obstructions.
   - (e) The height from which the escape is to be made.

11. *Swimming.*

    (a) Don't discard your clothing.

    (b) Swim slowly and steadily ; in any case your progress will be limited when wearing a life-saving waistcoat.

    (c) If you must swim through fire, jump feet first, upwind of the aircraft. Swim into the wind using the breaststroke, and try to make breathing holes by splashing the flames away from your head and arms. You may be able to swim under water, after first deflating your life-saving waistcoat.

    (d) If there is a danger of under-water explosions while you are in the water, the likelihood of injury will be reduced if you swim or float on your back.

12. *Final Hints.* In conclusion, stay with the aircraft and do not bale out, unless there is structural failure, uncontrollable fire, or the ditching characteristics of the aircraft are so poor as to make an attempted ditching extremely hazardous. If a ditching is inevitable and you have sufficient warning, it should be carried out while some use of power remains. Even when " K " type dinghies are carried, the advantages of a successful ditching are that the crew will be together, in a larger and more seaworthy dinghy ; they will be less exposed, with more equipment, and will be more easily seen from the air. In consequence, their morale and their chance of survival should be much greater.

## IMMEDIATE ACTIONS AFTER DITCHING

13. Immediately after a ditching, certain actions have to be carried out. These must be drilled until they become instinctive, and yet they must be flexible enough to cover such contingencies as injury or death of any member of the crew, which would necessitate one man doing the work of two in the precious seconds before the aircraft sinks. These immediate and subsequent actions are detailed in paras. 14 to 18.

14. *Release and Board the Dinghy.* Inflate the dinghies and get aboard, as laid down in the drill. Don't jump in or you may damage the dinghy. Don't board an inverted dinghy, for if the air beneath is expelled a suction is created and the dingy may be difficult to right (see Fig. 1). Make sure that all the survival equipment goes aboard, especially a parachute pack, which is probably the most valuable single piece of survival equipment. With a little ingenuity it can be made to serve a multitude of purposes, especially in the clothing line.

**15.** *Roll Call.* The captain of each dinghy calls the roll, endeavours to find any missing crew or passengers, and then cuts the painter. Thus it can be seen that in a passenger-carrying aircraft the complement of each dinghy should be clearly defined before take-off.

**16.** *Paddle Clear and Salvage Equipment.* Paddle clear of the aircraft. Beware of any jagged metal. Beware of the aircraft as it sinks, especially the tail plane. Salvage all floating equipment and lash all equipment securely to the dinghy. One of the occupants should then securely attach himself to the dinghy with a length of line—a safety precaution against losing the dinghy through it overturning and drifting away.

**17.** *Stream Sea Drogues and Service Dinghy.* Rendezvous with the other dinghy if more than one has been launched and secure the dinghies together. About twenty-five feet of line between dinghies has been found to be the best length to avoid snatching.

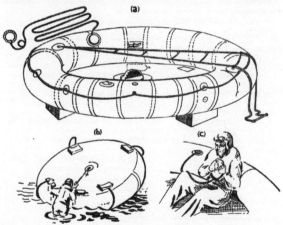

(a)

(b)          (c)

Fig. 1. TYPE "J" DINGHY
(a) Type "J" Dinghy     (b) Method of righting dinghy     (c) Topping-up

Stream the sea drogues to minimize dinghy drift. If necessary, top-up the buoyancy chamber using the topping-up bellows. Bale out with the baler and Viscose sponge. The sponge, which resembles a flat biscuit, will need plenty of soaking before it reaches its full size. If the sea is rough, rig the weather aprons to keep the occupants and the inside of the dinghy dry.

18. *Administer First Aid.* First aid should be administered without delay to the injured and to those suffering from shock. Injured personnel usually require extra water, food, and clothing, a point to be borne in mind when rationing. Wet clothes should be removed and dried, if you have spare clothing. In very cold weather, put on your protective clothing immediately if you are not already wearing it, otherwise you will be forced to keep on your wet clothing rather than risk exposure. That parachute silk will now come in handy for making improvised shirts, socks, and leggings, secured with pieces of shroud line. See paras. 26 to 28 for precautions against weather and details of dinghy ailments and first aid treatments.

## PLAN OF ACTION IN DINGHY

19. When the immediate actions after ditching have been completed, the captain should discuss a plan of action with the crew. If the captain is missing or badly injured it will be necessary to appoint another captain before trying to formulate the plan of action. Apart from easing the general tension, the discussion should serve to obtain the full agreement of the crew on all points of the plan. The points enumerated in para. 20 should be considered.

20. *Factors Affecting the Plan of Action.*

    (a) The state of W/T contact and the amount of information signalled before ditching.

    (b) The likelihood of air search and its probable efficiency in the prevailing weather.

    (c) The position of ditching in relation to the nearest land, surface craft, main shipping lanes, and air routes.

    (d) Knowledge of, and the advantage to be gained from, wind, current, and tides. This will be important in the tropics where air search may be limited in scope, and it may ultimately be decided to make a landfall.

    (e) Rations available, particularly water.

21. The decision must then be made on whether to remain in the vicinity of the ditching or to set course for an area where help is

more likely. Generally, it is preferable to remain in the vicinity of the ditching for at least 72 hours ; but should circumstances favour a departure from this area (*e.g.* proximity of land, shipping lanes, etc.) no time should be lost in getting " under way " so as to take advantage of the crew's initial fitness and energy. The plan of action should be adhered to, despite any temptation to change it later, for it was formulated when all were in a state of mind to think and plan coherently.

22. *Dinghy Log.* A log should be kept throughout the period in the dinghy. The first entry should include all details of the emergency : the names of survivors; date, time, and position of ditching; the behaviour of the aircraft at ditching and the length of time it remained afloat; weather conditions; items of equipment salvaged; and details of available rations. Later entries should include details of the dinghy's progress, notes on crew morale and physical condition, rations issued, weather, and aircraft sighted.

23. *Signalling Gear.* All signalling gear should be checked and prepared for instant use, according to the instructions supplied with each item. The following hints should enable you to make your signals more effective and help to conserve them.

(a) The life of the battery in " Walter " varies from about 20 hours continuous running in temperate conditions to 8 hours in tropical or arctic conditions. To conserve the battery, switch on the transmitter for periods of only 2 minutes at intervals of 5 minutes, except when an aircraft is heard or sighted, when it should be left on. When the aircraft has sighted and marked the dinghy's position and is homing a rescue surface craft, switch the transmitter on and off for 20-second periods.

(b) The Dinghy Radio S.C.R. 578 is your only W/T link, so transmit as long as your strength will allow, but you must transmit at the hour plus 10 to 20 minutes and 40 to 50 minutes. These periods will cover the listening watches of search aircraft, ships, and shore stations.

(c) Hold on to pyrotechnics until an aircraft is seen or heard, and do not expend them until certain of results. Aircraft searching for you at night will, weather permitting, fly between 3,000 and 5,000 feet, and will fire a single green pyrotechnic at intervals of 5 to 10 minutes depending on the ground speed and visibility. When you see the pyrotechnic fired by the aircraft, allow 30 seconds to elapse, then fire a red pyrotechnic, followed by a second one after a short interval. This second pyrotechnic enables the aircraft to check the alteration of course made towards you. Additional pyrotechnics need be fired only if the aircraft appears to be getting off course, and finally when it is almost overhead.

(*d*) Make sure all the crew can use the heliograph. When the sun is shining this is your best visual signalling device, and on a bright day the flash can be seen for 15 miles. The dinghy radio signal lamp can be used at night for automatic or manually keyed visual signals.

(*e*) Try to conserve your fluorescene sea marker. Although once it has been in the water it is supposed to be useless for a second time, it is not necessarily so. The main problem is to prevent it contaminating your food and water when it is brought aboard after having been wetted. To make the best use of the fluorescene marker, the following is suggested. If your W/T or R/T contact before ditching was good and your distress signals were acknowledged, allow sufficient time to elapse for search aircraft to reach the area, then stream the fluorescene block and leave it out. If your W/T or R/T contact before ditching was poor, stream the block only if an aircraft is seen or heard and bring it in again if you are not located.

(*f*) Remember that aircrew whistles can be used to help a man in the water to locate the dinghy, or in an attempt to attract the attention of passing surface craft.

## ALLOCATION OF DUTIES

24. Duties should be allotted by the captain to all occupants of the dinghy. This will help to prevent those mental disturbances, indicated perhaps by outbursts of temper over trivial matters, which are likely to arise as a result of apprehension and exhaustion. In any case, these duties will be invaluable to your plan of survival.

25. Duties should include signaller, navigator, aircraft spotter, and fisherman, and in a large crew can be rotated by means of a watch system. A record of duties carried out should be entered in the log, which is kept by the captain and his second-in-command. The duty of distributing the rations is the sole responsibility of the captain, the issues being recorded in the log to avoid arguments.

26. *Hot Climates.* In hot climates some form of sun shelter should be erected in the dinghy, care being taken to avoid any restriction of air round the occupants. Unnecessary clothing should be discarded, but the whole body should remain covered with one thin layer of material. The head and neck should always be kept covered. During the day, clothing should be worn soaked in sea-water, but it should be dried out thoroughly before sundown. Eyes should be protected from sunlight and reflected glare by wearing sun glasses or improvised eye shields. As a precaution against sunburn, which can occur even in cloudy weather, the anti-sunburn cream from the first aid packs should be used. Mild exercise, involving slow and easy movements of the limbs, should be taken, but over exertion should be avoided. Every precaution should be observed against sunstroke and heat exhaustion.

27. *Cold Climates.* In cold climates it is essential to keep oneself and the inside of the dinghy as dry as possible. All wet clothing should be removed and dried, if dry clothing is available; otherwise dampness should be reduced as far as possible by squeezing the wet clothing. A wind break should be rigged, and loose articles of clothing or a parachute wrapped round the body. There should also be adequate insulation against the cold floor of the dinghy. So that body heat may be transmitted to persons suffering from cold, occupants should lie together in the bottom of the dinghy. Hands can be warmed under arm-pits, between thighs, etc. Mild exercise should be taken to prevent stiffness of muscles and joints, and face muscles should be exercised frequently to ward off frost-bite.

## PROTECTION OF HEALTH

28. The ailments likely to be suffered by survivors at sea are chiefly caused by exposure to weather and sea-water, and by shortage of fresh water.

    (a) *Seasickness.* The performance of duties requiring some concentration helps to ward off seasickness. Its treatment is to refrain from eating and drinking for some time, to lie still, and to maintain bodily warmth. Anti-seasickness tablets are provided in the larger first aid kits.

    (b) *Immersion Foot.* Exposure of legs and feet to cold water for some time results in damage to the tissues. The affected part becomes red and painful and difficult to move. This is followed by swelling, the appearance of blisters and dark patches, and breaks in the skin. Prevention lies in keeping the feet as warm and dry as possible, and in ensuring that the floor of the dinghy is dry. The toes and feet should be moved frequently to assist blood circulation, and tightly fitting boots should be discarded. Remedial action is to remove footwear ; wrap feet in loose, dry articles of clothing or strips of parachute ; raise the feet clear of any water ; and keep the body warm. The affected parts should not be rubbed. " Everhot " bags should on no account to placed near the affected limb ; they may, however, be used to maintain bodily warmth.

(c) *Salt Water Sores.* These are boils or " burns " caused by exposure to salt water. Prevention is by keeping the body as dry as possible. The sores should be cleaned but not squeezed, and sulphanilamide crystals should be applied. Large sores should be covered with a dressing.

(d) *Sore Eyes.* Sore eyes result from excessive exposure to glare from the sky and water, and should be treated with boracic ointment and bandaged lightly. In the absence of a suitable ointment, a damp bandage should be applied.

(e) *Parched Lips and Cracked Skin.* These discomforts may be remedied by the application of any greasy ointment, such as boracic or vaseline.

(f) *Constipation or Difficult Urination.* These complaints should not give cause for alarm, as they are to be expected with a shortage of food and fresh water.

(g) *Frost-Bite.* The symptoms of frost-bite consist of small patches of white or cream coloured skin, stiff and firm to the touch. A prickling sensation may be felt. If the condition is allowed to become serious, tissues and bone may become frozen and blood-cells clot. When the affected part is warmed, there will be a swelling and redness of the skin with accompanying pain depending on the degree of frost-bite. Frost-bite is usually experienced in extreme cold ; exposed fingers, nose, and ears being most susceptible. Protection is obtained by keeping as warm and dry as possible, moving limbs, and exercising face muscles. Affected parts must not be rubbed or massaged, but warmed gently with breath, warm hands, or other warm parts of the body. The precautions to be observed against the direct heat of " Everhot " bags are the same as for immersion foot.

## DANGEROUS FISH

29. Dangerous fish, such as the shark, barracuda, and swordfish, are most common in tropical waters. Without provocation, they will not normally attack you or the dinghy. However, a brief description of these fish, together with a few simple hints, should help to safeguard you from attack or injury.

30. *Sharks.* Ocean sharks have the power to kill, but in the tropics, where their food is abundant, they are not normally ferocious. They are cowards and can usually be frightened off by the jab of a stick, a blow struck with the fist or a knife, particularly at the nose, or by the splash of water. Making a commotion in the water, however, may attract sharks from a distance. The tiger shark can be identified by the black stripes on its dorsal fin and sides ; natives do not regard it as more savage than other sharks. Reef and lagoon sharks are much smaller, ranging up to only four or five feet long. They are considered harmless by the natives, but they may snap at you if they are allowed to come too close. The only shark of which the Polynesians are really afraid is the *niuhi*, or man-eating shark, which will sometimes attack without provocation (Fig. 2). Fortunately it lives in deep water and rarely comes to the surface. It can be identified by its dark blue dorsal fin and back, and its stubby tail. The tails of other sharks have a long upper lobe.

Fig. 2. MAN-EATING SHARK

31. *Barracuda.* The barracuda is aggressive and is similar in appearance to a pike, except that it has two large dorsal fins in line on its back. Its rather elongated body and long pointed jaws should help you to recognize it.

**32. Swordfish.** There are many varieties of large fish, similar to the swordfish, all possessing a long bill or sword with which they attack shoals of small fish for food. They are not normally dangerous unless attacked or wounded, when they have been known to ram a boat (Fig. 3).

Fig. 3. SWORDFISH

**33. Wading Dangers.** If putting ashore or wading in search of food, especially in the tropics, be careful where you put your hands and feet. Apart from wounds which may be inflicted by coral, there is always the danger from eels such as the Moray eel, sting-rays, and poisonous shellfish (Figs. 4 and 7). See also paras. 52 to 54 on poisonous fish.

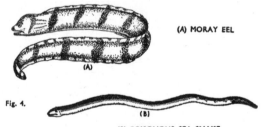

(A) MORAY EEL

Fig. 4.

(B) POISONOUS SEA SNAKE

**34. Hints on Dealing with Dangerous Fish.**

   (a) Keep clothing on and keep a good look out.

   (b) Do not fish if sharks, barracuda, or swordfish are in the vicinity.

(c) Do not trail hands or feet over the side of the dinghy.

(d) Do not throw waste food or scraps overboard during the daytime.

(e) If dangerous fish are about, remain quiet, and the likelihood of attack will be negligible.

(f) Survivors in the water without a dinghy should form a circle facing outwards and beat the water with strong regular strokes, if sharks are about.

## DRINKING WATER

35. Drinking water is your most essential need. A man in good health can live from 20 to 30 days without food ; without water he can live only for about 10 days, and even less in the tropics. A man needs a minimum of a pint (20 ounces) a day to keep fit, but he can survive on two to eight ounces a day. Therefore *the rationing of water must be instituted without delay and not relaxed until final rescue.*

36. *Water Rationing.* The sources of water in your emergency packs and survival kits are made up of sea water de-salting apparatus, and tins, bottles, or cushions containing fresh water. A still may also be included. The de-salting apparatus and still should be used first, while you still have the mental ability and patience to cope with them. A plastic drinking cup is provided, marked in nine divisions of approximately two ounces each, and should be used for rationing. While no hard and fast rules can be laid down for the rationing of water, the following method is recommended :—

(a) *1st Day.* No water issued, except for the injured. The body acts as a reservoir and you can live off the water it has stored.

(b) *2nd, 3rd, and 4th Days.* 14 ounces per head daily, if available.

(c) *5th Day Onwards.* Two to eight ounces per head daily, depending on the climate and the water available. Rain water, and water obtained from any additional source, must also be rationed, except while it is raining as explained in para. 38

37. When drinking, the lips, mouth, and throat should be moistened before swallowing.

**38. *Rain Water.*** For survival over a prolonged period, especially in the tropics, you will be dependent on rain for your drinking water. You must always be prepared to improvise a rain trap with the dinghy weather apron, at the first sign of rain. The salt should be washed off the apron with the first rain water collected, and then all possible containers should be filled. At the same time, drink your fill slowly and deeply. Don't drink quickly after being on short rations, or you may vomit.

**39. *Icebergs.*** Icebergs are a potential source of drinking water in polar latitudes, but extreme caution should be exercised in approaching them. In the lower latitudes icebergs are usually well eroded and should be avoided, as they are liable to overturn without warning. The flat-topped icebergs and the small " growlers " of the higher latitudes are safe to approach.

**40. *Old Sea Ice.*** Sea ice is of two main types. Young sea ice is salty, like the water from which it was formed, but after a year it loses its salt and becomes almost fresh. Old sea ice can be distinguished by its smooth rounded corners and bluish colour. Young sea ice is rougher and milky-grey in colour. In summer, drinking water can be obtained from pools in the old sea ice or from melting brash ice floating in the vicinity.

**41. *Immersion of the Body.*** It is possible to reduce your thirst by immersion of the body in the sea, although you must remain in the water for an hour or more to gain any real benefit. Immersion will be most beneficial in the tropics—if sharks are not present. Above latitude 50 deg., the coldness of the water is likely to do more harm than good.

**42. *Fish Juices.*** Experiments have been made to squeeze the juice from fish and use it as a water substitute, but without any great success. It has also been advocated that fish could be cut into cubes and chewed for the moisture content. General opinion, however, is no longer in favour of these methods, as it is considered that additional fresh water would be necessary to assimilate the protein in the fish juices. Furthermore, it would require a fish of about 20 pounds to produce a pint of juice.

## WATER RULES

**43.** To preserve the water in the body is almost as important as having water to drink, so here are a few very important rules for guidance :—

(a) ***Keep your shirt on,*** in every sense, to prevent the
loss of body moisture through unnecessary perspiration
and exposure. Rig up some sort of awning, but not so as
to restrict the cooling effect of the breeze. When the sun
gets up, keep the clothing wet with sea water, the evaporation of which will cool the body, but discontinue if chilliness
results. Rinse accumulations of salt from the clothing so
that the skin will not be harmed. In the later afternoon,
allow the clothing to dry ready for the night.

(b) ***Sleep and rest*** are most important during a shortage of
water. In the tropics, keep your exercise to a minimum.
The body relies on the evaporation of sweat to keep its
temperature constant and, if you keep moving around,
it is possible to lose up to two quarts of body moisture in
a day.

(c) ***Prevent seasickness if possible.*** Valuable water
can be lost through being sick. Seasickness tablets are
contained in the larger dinghy first aid outfits, and should
be taken at the first feeling of sickness.

(d) ***Do not drink sea water,*** or attempt to make your fresh
water last longer by adding sea water to it. It will only
increase your thirst and make you violently sick.

(e) ***Do not drink urine.*** It is injurious and will only decrease
your resistance and increase your thirst.

(f) ***Do not drink alcohol.*** It will nauseate you and increase
your thirst by drawing water from the intestines and
kidneys, and may give you convulsions. Alcohol has no
thirst-quenching value and is dangerous to drink in these
circumstances.

(g) ***Keep smoking to a minimum.*** Smoking increases
thirst, and smokers should be encouraged to cut it out or to
reserve smoking for the night watches, when they will find
it more soothing and less likely to make them thirsty.

(h) ***To allay thirst,*** and keep the mouth moist by increasing
saliva, it may be found beneficial to suck on a piece of
cloth or a button. Chewing gum may help, but it sometimes has the effect of increasing thirst.

(j) *Do not eat unless you have adequate water for digestion.* Water and food in survival are closely related. In the following section on food, it is explained that the amount of drinking water available determines the type and quantity of food which may be eaten.

# FOOD

44. In the adverse conditions of survival at sea, it is vital to realize that the amount of the water ration will determine how much food may be eaten and of what it should consist, for the body requires water for the digestion of food and the elimination of waste products. Food can be divided into two main categories, so far as the balance between food and water is concerned. These are :—

(a) *Carbohydrate foods, i.e.* sugars and starches, which require very little water. Represented by potatoes, fruits, and the food tablets and sweets in the emergency flying rations.

(b) *Protein foods,* which require a large amount of water. Represented by meat, fish, shellfish, eggs, and certain green leaf vegetables including seaweed.

45. *Food and Water Rules.* As far as the survivor at sea or the castaway is concerned, it is sufficient to follow three simple rules :—

(a) The quantity of the food and water rations must be varied in direct proportion to each other. If you have plenty of water you can increase the food ration, but as the water ration decreases the food ration must also be decreased.

(b) Protein food, such as any raw fish, bird, or seaweed, will require more water than your emergency flying rations.

(c) Live off natural foods if your ration of water will permit, and save your emergency flying rations for the real emergency when your water supply is getting low.

## Emergency Flying Rations

46. There are two types of ration, each containing carbohydrate foods, and therefore invaluable for sustaining you when your water ration is low. The Type " P " ration contains peanut toffee ; the Mark 3 contains malted milk tablets, barley sugar, chewing gum, and energy tablets. Each personal survival kit should contain one of each of these, and the aircraft's emergency pack should contain one Mark 3 ration per man.

47. No hard and fast rule for rationing can be given, but a minimum of four malted milk tablets or their equivalent in peanut toffee per day is sufficient to sustain life. The barley sugar can be used occasionally to relieve the monotony of this diet. At this minimum ration, one tin of rations will last one man approximately 12 days and your rationing scheme can therefore be planned accordingly.

## Fish

48. Fish represent your largest possible source of natural food and the great majority of fish are edible. In the tropics, a rough and ready rule is that the fish of the open sea, out of sight of land, are safe to eat, whereas some of the fish caught in lagoons may not only be poisonous to eat but poisonous to handle (see paras. 52 to 54).

49. The flesh of fish is valuable food, but remember that it can be included in your diet only when you have sufficient water for its digestion, roughly two parts of water to one of fish.

50. If you have more fish than you require, it can be dried in the sun for future use. This will probably make it more palatable, but dried fish, flesh, or entrails should not be eaten unless your water ration is at least 30 ounces per day.

51. *Fishing—Useful Hints.*

    (a) Do not handle the fishing line with bare hands or fasten it to the dinghy. Use gloves or a cloth when handling fish, for even non-poisonous fish may have extremely sharp fins or gill covers.

    (b) If using a spoon or spinner, keep it moving, either by casting out and retrieving hand over hand, or by letting it down as far as the line will allow and again retrieving it, or by jigging at various depths.

    (c) Having caught a fish, you can cut its skin or flesh into strips with which to bait the hooks or spinners. The eyes and entrails also make good bait.

    (d) Do not fish in or near large shoals, as large fish (*e.g.* shark or barracuda) may be feeding from them.

    (e) A light at night attracts fish and is therefore an aid to fishing.

    (f) Surplus fish can be cut into strips and dried for future use as food or bait. It should last a few days.

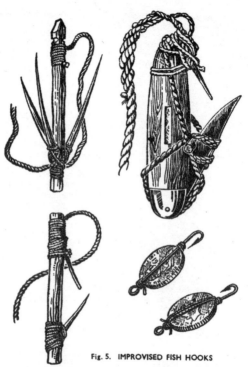

Fig. 5. IMPROVISED FISH HOOKS

(g) A dinghy often attracts small fish, which make excellent bait. A dip net can be improvised in order to catch them. If they can be caught in sufficient quantities these small fish also make excellent food.

**(h)** A piece of cloth or wool, especially if it is red in colour, is a good substitute for bait. A tuft of hair or a white feather tied to the shank of the hook will often serve the same purpose. Some improvised fish hooks are illustrated in Figs. 5 and 6.

## Poisonous Fish

52. Most fish are edible, palatable, and wholesome. However, there are a few with flesh that is poisonous and others with poisonous spines which are dangerous to handle.

53. Most of the fish with poisonous flesh are to be found in tropical waters. Their chief characteristic is that they lack ordinary scales, and instead have either a naked skin, or are encased in a bony box-like covering, or are covered with bristles, spiny scales, strong sharp thorns, or spines. Others puff up like a balloon on being taken out of the water. If you are ashore, remember that cooking does not destroy the poisonous alkaloids in these fish. Finally never eat a fish that has slimy gills, sunken eyes, flabby flesh or skin, or an unpleasant odour. If on pressing the

Fig. 6. IMPROVISED FISH HOOKS

thumb against the fish it remains deeply dented, the fish is probably stale and should not be eaten. Good flesh should be firm and not slimy.

54. Fish which are dangerous to handle have sharp spines on their heads, tails, or fins. These spines may cause a burning or stinging, or even an agonizing pain which is out of all proportion to the apparent severity of the wound. The pain is caused by the venom injected by the spines, which in some cases can be very dangerous if not fatal. These fish are usually either yellowish-grey or black in colour, often having patches of red or orange that give them a mottled appearance. Avoid all types of jelly fish, rays that have a diamond shaped body and long tail, and sea snakes. Sea snakes should be fairly easily distinguished from eels because, unlike eels, they have long plates or scales covering their bodies and heads, and compressed flattened tails. Sea snakes are normally found only in inshore tropical waters (Figs. 4 and 7).


## Seaweeds

55. Most seaweeds are edible and, either raw or cooked, form a valuable addition to your diet, providing your water ration is adequate, for they tend to make you thirsty. Seaweeds are found mainly in inshore waters, but some of the seaweeds floating on the open ocean are good to eat. The following simple rules should be observed :—

(a) Fresh, healthy specimens have no marked odour or flavour and are firm and smooth to the touch. If the plant is wilted and slimy and has a fishy smell, it is decaying and should not be eaten.

(b) Do not eat the threadlike or slender branched forms. They are not poisonous, but may contain irritating acids. You can detect this by crushing some with your hands, when the released acid will cause the plant to decay so rapidly that within five minutes it will give off an offensive odour.

(c) Inspect the seaweed for small, stinging organisms which may be living in it. Crabs, shrimps, and small fish are often found attached to the seaweed and can be shaken off into the dinghy.

SCORPION FISH

PORQUPINE FISH

TOADFISH

STONEFISH

FILEFISH

STINGRAY

ZEBRA FISH

Fig. 7.  POISONOUS AND VENOMOUS FISH

## Birds

56. All sea birds are edible, either raw or cooked, though some may taste a little peculiar. They are scarce in the open ocean, more than 100 miles from land. The most characteristic of the ocean birds are the albatross, with a wing span of from six to twelve feet, and the petrel and hooked-beaked shearwater, which are about the size of a large pigeon. They can be caught, although not easily, by trolling a floating bait. A large fish hook could be used, but a gorge in the shape of a diamond, about four inches by one inch or more, floating on the surface, and completely covered by fish as bait, is probably more successful. The bird gets the gorge wedged in its throat after swallowing the bait (Fig. 8).


## MAKING A LANDFALL

57. *Introduction.* The chances are odds-on that you will be found and rescued within four or five days. In time of war, sailing dinghies are used to enable ditched crews to head out to sea if they are uncomfortably close to an enemy held coastline. In peacetime, however, as has already been stated, you should put out the drogue and stay near the scene of ditching as long as possible. This will help the aircraft searching for you and increase the chance of your eventual rescue. However, you may have ditched in a remote part of the ocean where air and sea search is sparse, and this, together with other conditions, such as favourable trade winds or ocean currents, may ultimately lead you to try to make a landfall. The details of jungle, desert, and arctic survival are dealt with in the other pamphlets of this series, but somewhat special conditions apply to the dry islands and atolls of the Indo-Pacific ocean area, where a landfall may be made (see paras. 62 to 63). These dry islands, as the name suggests, are islands where the rainfall is insufficient for normal vegetation, but where men can at least rest before continuing their journey, or even exist if necessary until rescued.

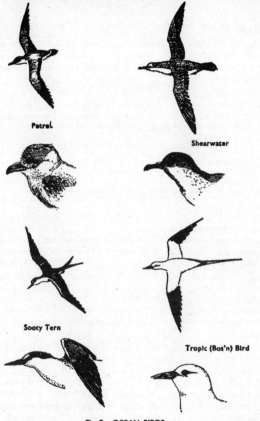

Petrel

Shearwater

Sooty Tern

Tropic (Bos'n) Bird

Fig. 8. OCEAN BIRDS

58. **Wind and Currents.** The movement of the dinghy will be mainly governed by the prevailing winds and ocean currents, and these can be utilized intelligently to make a landfall. The following points should be borne in mind :—

(a) The lower the dinghy rides in the water, and the lower its occupants sit or lie, the greater will be the effect of the current. This effect can be increased by the use of the drogue.

(b) On the other hand, if the wind is favourable the dinghy should be lightened as much as possible. Survivors should sit as erect as possible to increase the wind effect, and any sort of makeshift sail will help. The drogue should be hauled inboard, and the water ballast pockets tripped.

59. **Navigation and Direction at Sea.** If you are in a large dinghy with the remainder of your crew, and have your navigation equipment with you, so much the better. However, you may be alone, or without navigation equipment. If so, the following hints will help you to determine and maintain your course towards land or the shipping lanes :—

(a) If you have no compass, remember that the sun rises approximately in the east and sets in the west. If you are north of latitude 23½ deg. N., the sun will pass to the *south* of you in its path across the sky. South of latitude 23½ deg. S. it will pass to the *north* of you. Between these latitudes the sun's path varies with the time of year. The direction in which the sun rises is shown in the table below.

## SUNRISE TABLE

DIRECTION IN WHICH SUN RISES — DEGREES EAST OF TRUE NORTH

*Direction measured when top of sun just shows above horizon*

| Latitude | Mar. 21 | May 5 | June 22 | Aug. 9 | Sept. 23 | Nov. 7 | Dec. 22 | Feb. 5 |
|---|---|---|---|---|---|---|---|---|
| 60° North .. | 89° | 55° | 37° | 55° | 89° | 122° | 140° | 122° |
| 30° North .. | 90° | 71° | 63° | 71° | 90° | 108° | 116° | 108° |
| 0° (Equator) .. | 90° | 74° | 67° | 74° | 90° | 106° | 113° | 106° |
| 30° South .. | 90° | 72° | 64° | 72° | 90° | 104° | 117° | 109° |

(b) Between sunrise and sunset, and north and south of the latitudes shown in the table, an approximate indication of direction can be obtained by using a watch. Point the hour hand at the sun, and a point on the watch dial halfway between the hour hand and twelve o'clock will indicate the approximate direction of true south if you are in the northern hemisphere, or of true north if you are in the southern hemisphere. In the tropics the method is unreliable.

(c) At night, if the sky is clear, reliable indications of direction can be obtained from the stars. In the northern hemisphere, true north can be ascertained from the constellation of the Great Bear, which points to Polaris (North Star), the star over the north pole. In the southern hemisphere, the Southern Cross indicates the direction of south. Other constellations, such as Orion, rise in the east and set in the west, moving to the south of you when you are north of the equator and *vice versa*. (See Figs. 9 to 11.)

(d) Trying to estimate your latitude by measuring the angle of Polaris above the horizon will give you only a very approximate result unless you have a sextant and tables, for even if you were able to estimate the angle to within five degrees you could still be 300 nautical miles in error.

(e) Between the equatorial belt of very light and variable winds, known as the "Doldrums", and the latitudes 30 deg. N. and 30 deg. S., the prevailing winds are the north-east and south-east trades respectively. These winds are a boon to navigation, being very steady both in direction and speed, although they are subject to certain seasonal variations. From latitude 40 deg. N. and S. towards the poles the winds are mainly westerly.

60. The above are only general hints. Learn as much as you can by observation and questions about the winds and sea currents in the areas in which you operate. Learn to pick out the stars that have been mentioned and many more. That is how the first navigators found their way, and without navigational instruments it is still the best.

61. *Land Indications.* Native fishermen whose small canoes are blown out to sea often turn up days later none the worse for their experience. They keep on with their fishing, catch birds, and quench their thirst with rain water caught during the frequent

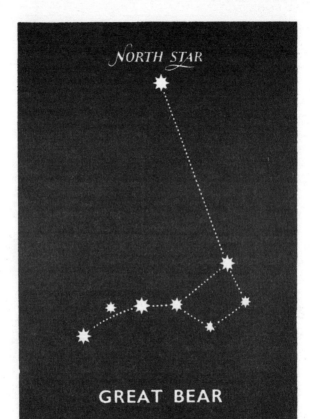

NORTH STAR

GREAT BEAR

SOUTHERN CROSS

CROSS

FALSE

CROSS

S

SOUTHERN CROSS

Fig. 10.  SOUTHERN CROSS                    Fig. 29

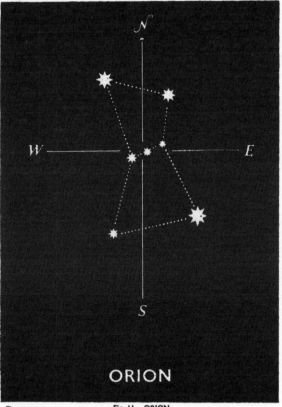

ORION

Fig. 11.  ORION

squalls. They often detect the presence of an island long before it can be seen, by one of the following methods :—

(a) Cumulus clouds in an otherwise clear sky are likely to have been formed over land.

(b) Very few sea birds sleep on the water, and very rarely do they fly more than 100 miles from land. The recognition of these birds and their direction of flight will often indicate the direction and distance of land. They fly away from land before noon and return in the late afternoon and evening. Storms sometimes blow land-based birds far out to sea, so that a lone bird is not a reliable indication.

(c) Lagoon glare ; a greenish tint in the sky or on the underside of a cloud caused by the reflection of sunlight from the shallow water over coral reefs.

(d) Drifting wood or vegetation is often a sign of the proximity of land.

## LIVING ON LAND

62. *Water.* Many islands in the Indo-Pacific area have a good water supply, while others do not. On a dry island, water fit to drink can be obtained by digging a hole in a depression about 100 yards above the high tide mark. The water may be brackish, so go no deeper than is necessary : normally it will be sufficient to dig a foot deeper after the first water starts to seep through. The fresh water, being less dense, will float on top, so " skim " off the fresher water from the top of your well with a shell. Large scallop-type shells will also be found useful in digging the well. If the water is very brackish, try a new hole somewhere else. Even brackish water in very limited quantities will not sicken you, and will help to keep you alive. When you have dug a suitable well, line the hole with coral slabs or pieces of rock to prevent the sand from caving in.

63. *Food on Dry Islands.* Seafood is the principal source of food on the dry islands of the Indo-Pacific area. Rats are usually the only mammals found on them, and edible vegetation is limited to one or two species. A list of the various foods is given below.

(a) *Seafood.* Look for clams, mussels, sea cucumbers, crabs, crayfish, shrimps, and sea urchins. They will be found along the shore and in pockets formed by the coral reefs (see Figs. 12 and 13). Beware of the poisonous varieties of shellfish, with cone-shaped or pointed spindle-shaped shells. Shellfish can be eaten raw, but it is safer to

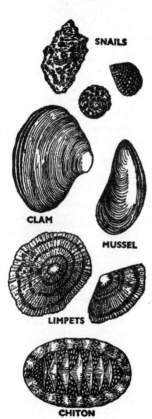

SNAILS

CLAM

MUSSEL

LIMPETS

CHITON

cook them. One very simple way is to cover them with sand or earth and build a fire over the pile, when they will cook in their own juices. Another way is to drop them into boiling water.

(b) *Fish.* Fishing with hook and line has been dealt with in para. 51. Fish can often be found in pools on reefs or among rocks at low tide. If there are no natural pools on the reefs, try a fish trap. Fig. 14 shows two types of fish traps. In the maze type the trap should be about 8 feet across with a mouth about 1½ feet wide, through which walls project two feet into the trap. It can be built with stones or stakes of wood. Fish that enter seldom find their way out.

(c) *Turtles.* Turtles breed on sandy shores and on small islands. They are all edible and their eggs are also an excellent source of nourishment. Follow the obvious trails made

Fig. 12. EDIBLE SEAFOOD

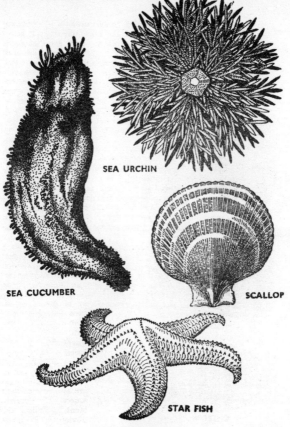

SEA URCHIN

SEA CUCUMBER

SCALLOP

STAR FISH

Fig. 13.  EDIBLE SEAFOOD

by sea turtles across the beach to find the places where the eggs are buried in the sand. When you have roughly determined the location of the eggs, prod the sand with a stick. Turtle eggs may be buried two feet deep and at a distance of about 20 yards from the water. They may be eaten raw but are much better boiled, although the white part remains watery. While spoiled eggs are to be avoided, those in an advanced state of incubation may be eaten if necessary. Turtles may be caught on the beach or on a reef. Rush them and turn them on their backs, but be careful of their jaws and claws. The neck can be pulled out and the throat cut or the entire head severed. Turtles are cleaned more easily after partial boiling or after cooking in a ground oven. Turtle steak and soup are luxuries and the blood is good food.

(d) *Pigweed or Purslane.* On barren atolls, the only readily edible vegetable food is the pigweed, a fleshy, soft-stemmed, reddish-green weed with yellow flowers, which stands 8 to 12 inches high and grows in large patches (see Fig. 15). It will relieve thirst, and tastes like watercress when eaten fresh and like slightly sour spinach when cooked. A diet of this plant, augmented by seafood, will sustain one indefinitely.

(e) *Pandanus or Screw Pine.* Less barren islands, having more soil and moisture, often support coconut palms and pandanus. The pandanus tree may be recognized by its palmlike trunk, heads of long spiny leaves, and aerial roots (see Fig. 16). The tender white flesh in the base of a head of young leaves may be eaten raw or cooked. The fruit, similar in size and appearance to the pineapple, is composed of segments or cones fixed to a soft core from

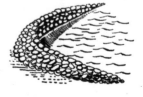

MAZE TYPE FISH TRAP     TIDAL FLAT FISH TRAP

Fig. 14. FISH TRAPS

which they readily separate when ripe. The ripe cones are orange yellow and very fragrant. Between the fibres and the soft inner part of the cones is lodged sugar and starch which may be extracted by chewing. After baking or roasting, scrape out the pulp with a shell or knife. The yellow paste can be eaten immediately or preserved by drying. The fruit is in season from June to October south of the equator. During the off season, the outer sides of the dry cones contain delicious kernels, which are lodged in small compartments in a hard shell. Cut off the fibrous end of the cone and place it on a flat rock, then crack it with a heavy stone held in both hands. Water can be obtained by tapping the tops of the aerial roots.

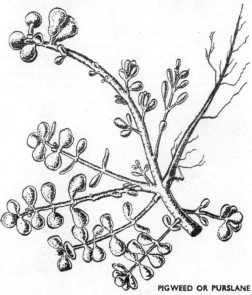

PIGWEED OR PURSLANE

Fig. 15

*(f)* ***Coconuts and the Coconut Palm.*** The coconut palm may be found on the less barren atolls, and is an ample provider of food. Each tree has nuts in all stages of growth. The green or yellowish-brown nuts contain excellent " milk " and " meat ". You can attempt to climb the tree in your bare feet using the rough rings of the bark as steps, or by tying a piece of cloth between your ankles

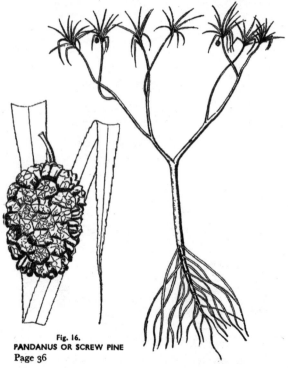

**Fig. 16.**
PANDANUS OR SCREW PINE

as a climbing bandage and hitching up the tree. Mature nuts can be picked up from the ground and are good to eat providing you can hear the milk inside when you shake them. The fibrous husk of the mature coconut can be prised off with a machete, but a husking stick of hard wood will do the job much better (see Fig. 17). To open a nut for drinking, pare off the soft outer shell at the pointed end with a machete or knife, then tap lightly around the end until a piece of hard shell about an inch or more in diameter is removed. Do not eat too much of the meat or drink too much of the milk of the mature nut, especially if you are in a weakened state, for you will find them very laxative.

**Fig. 17. BREAKING COCONUTS**

9/52 E43309/43693 Wt. 14965-BN.3592 10,800 12/53 Gp.8 F. & C. Ltd.

Fig. 18. RAF BASES 1958

Gibraltar
Luqa
Akrotiri
El Adam
Muharraq
Sharjah
Salalah
Masirah
Khormaksar
Kai Tak
Gan
Changi
Tengah
Seletar
Ascension
Island

Fig. 19. RAF GIBRALTAR

**Fig. 20. RAF CHANGI**

**Fig. 21. RAF GAN**

**Fig. 22. RAF CHRISTMAS ISLAND**

# Notes

....................................................................................

....................................................................................

....................................................................................

....................................................................................

....................................................................................

....................................................................................

....................................................................................

....................................................................................

....................................................................................

....................................................................................

....................................................................................

....................................................................................

....................................................................................

....................................................................................

....................................................................................

....................................................................................

....................................................................................

....................................................................................

# Notes

# Notes

# Notes

# Notes

# Notes

# Notes

......................................................................

......................................................................

......................................................................

......................................................................

......................................................................

......................................................................

......................................................................

......................................................................

......................................................................

......................................................................

......................................................................

......................................................................

......................................................................

......................................................................

......................................................................

......................................................................

......................................................................

......................................................................

......................................................................

# Notes

# Notes

# Notes

........................................................................
........................................................................
........................................................................
........................................................................
........................................................................
........................................................................
........................................................................
........................................................................
........................................................................
........................................................................
........................................................................
........................................................................
........................................................................
........................................................................
........................................................................
........................................................................
........................................................................
........................................................................
........................................................................
........................................................................

# Notes

# Notes

# Notes

........................................................................

........................................................................

........................................................................

........................................................................

........................................................................

........................................................................

........................................................................

........................................................................

........................................................................

........................................................................

........................................................................

........................................................................

........................................................................

........................................................................

........................................................................

........................................................................

........................................................................

........................................................................

........................................................................

........................................................................

# Notes

..............................................................
..............................................................
..............................................................
..............................................................
..............................................................
..............................................................
..............................................................
..............................................................
..............................................................
..............................................................
..............................................................
..............................................................
..............................................................
..............................................................
..............................................................
..............................................................
..............................................................
..............................................................
..............................................................
..............................................................

First issued to airmen in the 1950s, this reprint of The Air Ministry's Jungle Survival pamphlet includes emergency advice to crew operating over jungle regions.

Packed with original line drawings and instruction in:

- What to do if 'jungle hiking becomes boring'
- How to stay safe from poisonous reptiles and insects
- The benefits of using a 'fire thong'

# OUT NOW

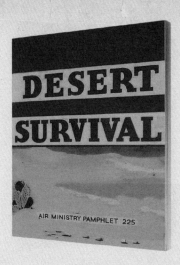

First issued to airmen in the 1950s, this reprint of The Air Ministry's
Desert Survival pamphlet includes emergency advice to crew
operating over desert regions.

Packed with original line drawings and instruction in:

- How to find water in a dry stream course

- How to make a hat out of seat cushions

# OUT NOW

First issued to airmen in the 1950s, this reprint of The Air Ministry's Arctic Survival pamphlet includes emergency advice to crew operating over arctic regions.

Packed with original line drawings and instruction in:

- The best faces to pull to prevent frostbite and, should you fail, when you can expect bits of you to 'fall off'

- How to build a structurally sound igloo

- How to fashion a mask to prevent snowblindness

# OUT NOW